zendoodle coloring BIG PICTURE

Magnificent Animals

Other great books in the series

zendoodle coloring

Big Picture: Birds & Butterflies
Big Picture: Calming Gardens
Big Picture: Mindful Inspirations

Baby Animals
Calming Swirls
Cozy Cats
Creative Sensations
Enchanting Gardens
Inspiring Zendalas
Into the Forest
Magical Fairies
Tranquil Gardens
Tropical Paradise
Under the Sea
Uplifting Inspirations
Winter Wonderland

zendoodle coloring **BIG PICTURE**

Tranquil Art for Experienced Eyes

Magnificent Animals

Illustrations by Deborah Muller

ST. MARTIN'S GRIFFIN
NEW YORK

ZENDOODLE COLORING BIG PICTURE: MAGNIFICENT ANIMALS.

Printed in the United States of America. For information, address
St. Martin's Press, 175 Fifth Avenue, New York, N.Y. 10010.

www.stmartins.com

ISBN 978-1-250-12140-0 (trade paperback)

Our books may be purchased in bulk for promotional, educational, or business use.
Please contact your local bookseller or the Macmillan Corporate and Premium
Sales Department at 1-800-221-7945, extension 5442, or by e-mail
at MacmillanSpecialMarkets@macmillan.com.

First Edition: November 2016

10 9 8 7 6 5 4 3 2 1